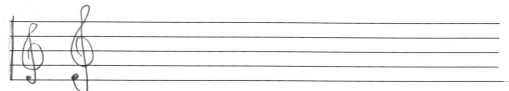

Darkness, 28th November 2017

> The still of winter, coming up to the stirring of the spring.

Psalm 89 — variations — a world built from compassion

Olam — one of the names of God — Essential goodness.

Chesed — loving kindness / compassion — no word for return

Yibaneh —

Tai-doi-dei — calling it the Divine — or the essential goodness.

Everything that exists is an expression of God's loving kindness

Deep winter — in the world of nature, the long night, Cold
All nature sleeps, + in the darkness lie the seeds of light
All life — the stillness of winter suspended

I will sleep in the dark-ness like a seed in the earth   Hey-yo hey-yo

Hebrew. Rabbi — for baby daughter born oct 9/11.    Olam loving kindness, no payback
Chesed יִב

|: Em  D  Cmaj7  D  Em :|
   G   D   ..    ..

(A) Olam chesed yibaneh, Tai-dai-dai ...

Olam chesed       di-di-dai dai i dai dai

(B) I will build this world from love, Tai dai dai dai dai
    And you must.. // And if we... / Then God will...

Instrumental — violin.

1 or 2 verses — unison

2 verses — 2 parts.
   a) as written
   b) piano solo/both/solo/both.

Take tambourine for someone to

2 more + add
   slow down at end

Printed in Great Britain
by Amazon